THE FABER EASY-PLAY KEYBOARD SERIES

Play Romantic ITALY

FABER MUSIC

Contents

© 1989 by Faber Music Ltd
First published in 1989 by Faber Music Ltd
3 Queen Square, London WC1N 3AU
Music drawn by Sambo Music Engraving
Cover design and typography by John Bury
Printed in England

Autumn (*The Seasons*) first movement

ANTONIO VIVALDI

Winter (*The Seasons*) slow movement

ANTONIO VIVALDI

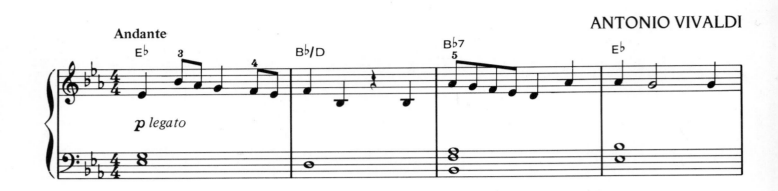

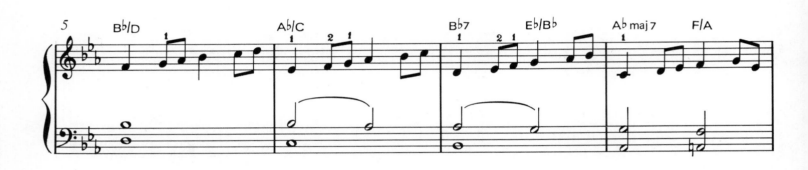

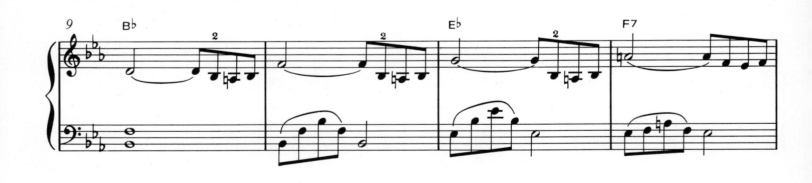

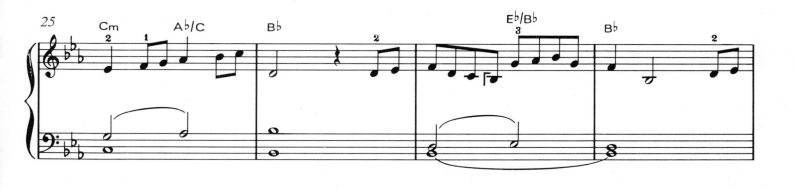

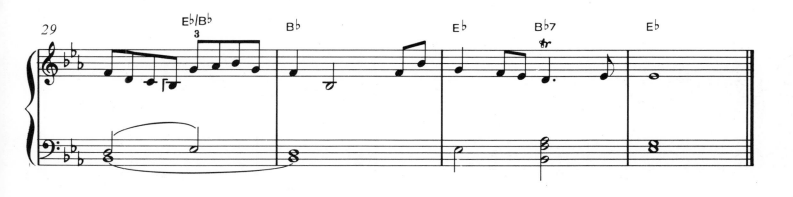

Autumn (*The Seasons*) last movement

ANTONIO VIVALDI

Minuet from String Quintet

Allegretto grazioso

LUIGI BOCCHERINI

Caprice No. 24

NICCOLÒ PAGANINI

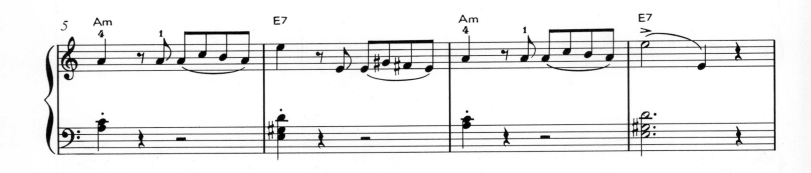

Overture (*William Tell*)

GIOACCHINO ROSSINI

Overture (*The Barber of Seville*)

GIOACCHINO ROSSINI

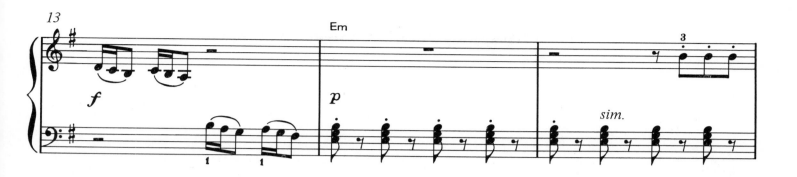

Overture (The Italian Girl in Algiers)

GIOACCHINO ROSSINI

Soldiers' Chorus (*Il Trovatore*)

GIUSEPPE VERDI

Triumphal March (*Aida*)

GIUSEPPE VERDI

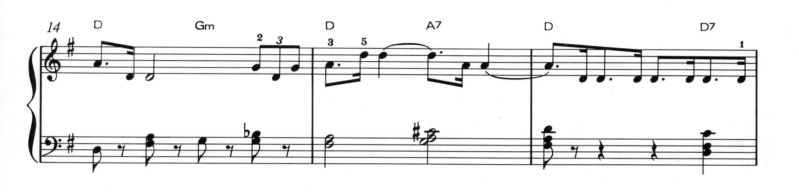

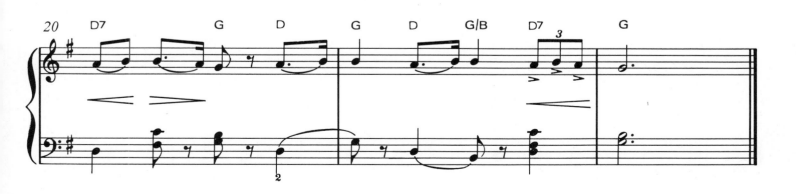

Drinking Song (*La Traviata*)

GIUSEPPE VERDI

La donna e mobile (Rigoletto)

GIUSEPPE VERDI

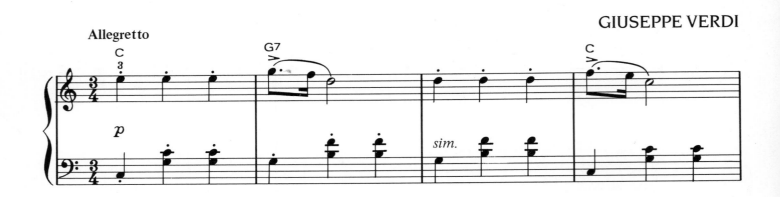

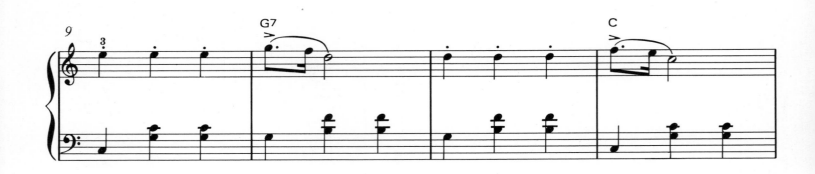

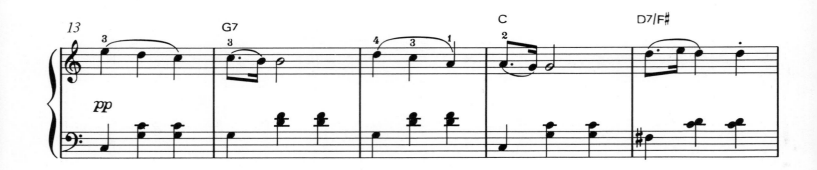

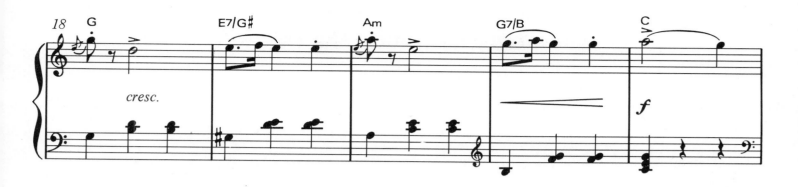

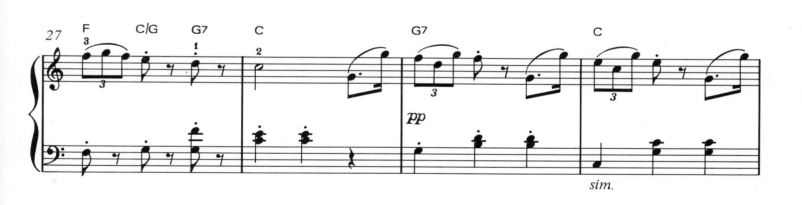

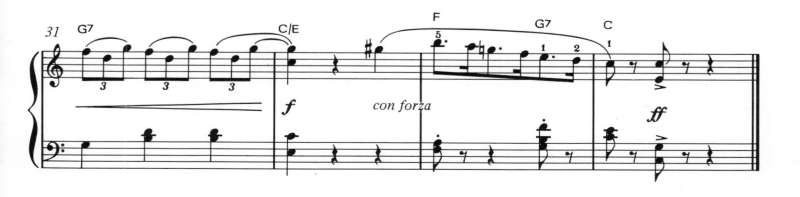

Theme from Prelude (*La Traviata*)

GIUSEPPE VERDI

Overture (*La forza del destino*)

GIUSEPPE VERDI

Ne andro lontana (La Wally)

ALFREDO CATALANI

21

On with the motley (*Pagliacci*)

RUGGIERO LEONCAVALLO

O sole mio

Di Capua

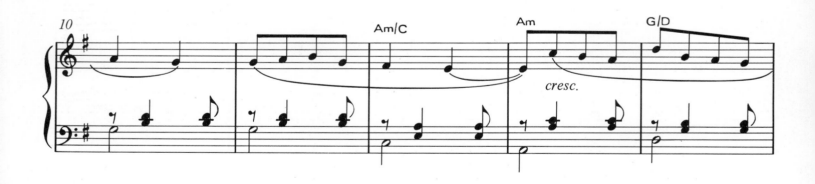

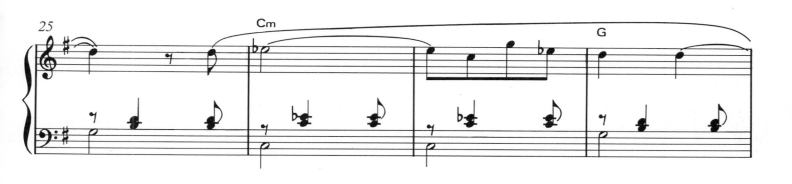

Your tiny hand is frozen (*La Bohème*)

GIACOMO PUCCINI

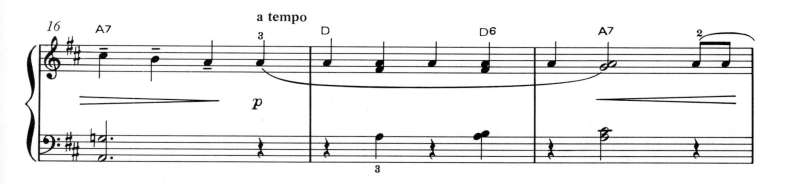

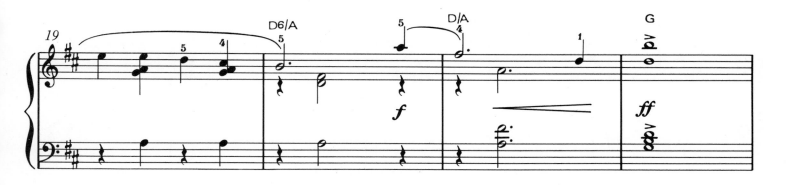

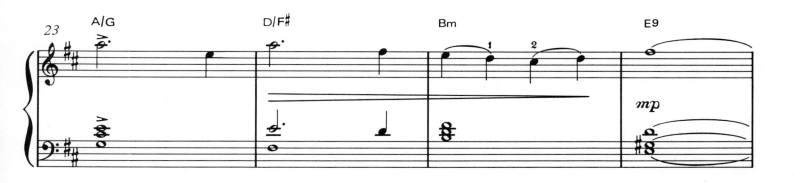

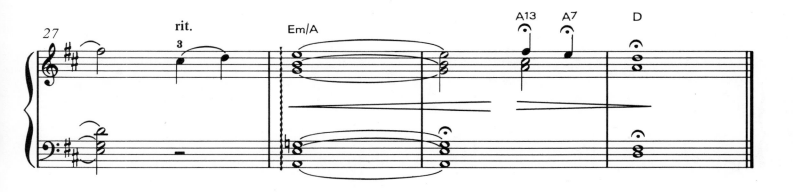

Musetta's Waltz Song (*La Bohème*)

GIACOMO PUCCINI

E *lucevan le stelle* (Tosca)

GIACOMO PUCCINI

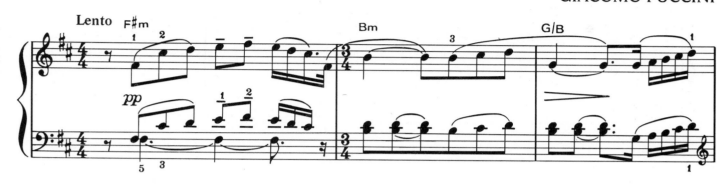

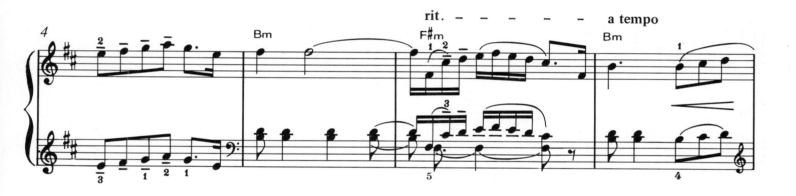

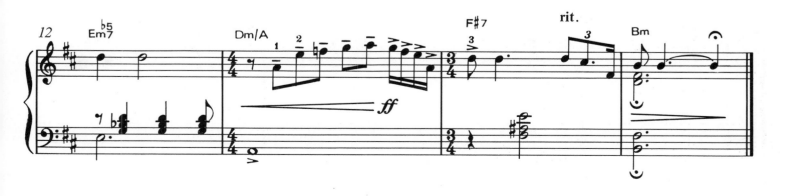

Humming Chorus (*Madama Butterfly*)

GIACOMO PUCCINI

One fine day (*Madama Butterfly*)

GIACOMO PUCCINI

Vissi d'arte (Tosca)

GIACOMO PUCCINI

None shall sleep (*Turandot*)

GIACOMO PUCCINI

O my beloved father (*Gianni Schicchi*)

GIACOMO PUCCINI